Personal Development

TABLE OF CONTENTS

Cover Art by
Matthew Archambault

Black & White Illustrations by
Ken Landgraf

EDCON
Publishing Group

Copyright © 2006
AV Concepts Corporation
Edcon Publishing Group

info@edconpublishing.com
1-888-553-3266   Fax 1-888-518-1564
30 Montauk Blvd., Oakdale NY 11769
www.edconpublishing.com

Printed in U.S.A.
ISBN# 1-55576-383-9

HOW TO GET
GOOD GRADES

During class, a message came over the loudspeaker: "Attention! Attention! Because of poor academic performance, the following students are not eligible to participate in extra-curricular activities for the remainder of the semester:

> Tim Martin
> Sue Riggs
> Hal Sachs…"

So you've learned that you'll have to attend summer school to improve your achievement. Perhaps someone has said, "I'm sorry, but you won't be graduating this year with your friends. You failed two required subjects, and you must repeat them."

Let's see what we can do about this.

One night Hal and Tim went to a little party over at Mel's house. Tim said to Mel, "Hey, this is a great party. I'm glad your parents aren't home. Where's Lara tonight, Mel?"

Mel answered, "We have a science test tomorrow, Tim. And you know Lara…if there's a test, she's got to study for it."

Tim sighed. "I studied all week because my mom said she'd give me fifty bucks if I got an A. But I'll probably get my usual D."

"Well, Tim," answered Mel, "I don't care what I get. I'm just going to party."

A few days later the students received their test results. "Hey!" grumbled Mel. "I knew the stuff, the teacher just didn't ask the right questions."

"I failed!" said Hal. "Why does everything happen to me?"

Lara smiled. "An A+. What a relief! I knew I could do it."

HOW TO GET GOOD GRADES

Sound familiar? I'm sure you've heard these same comments from your friends. Why is it that some students get *good* grades, and others *fail*?

School achievement is somewhat like mixing a cake. You have to have the right ingredients and know what to do with them.

Four ingredients that are needed for school achievement are:

1. **Education as a Value**
2. **Relevancy**
3. **Learning Skills**
4. **Motivation**

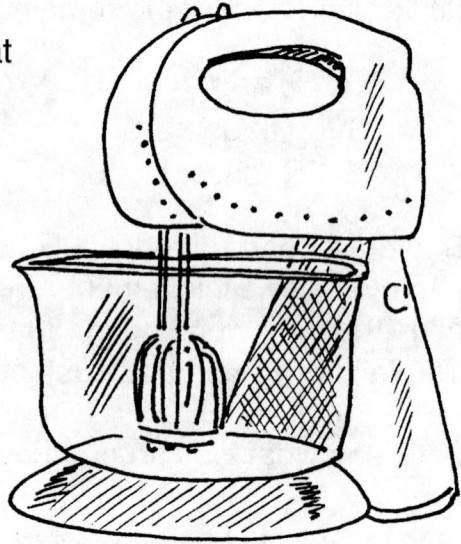

Let's examine our ingredients one at a time.

INGREDIENT #1

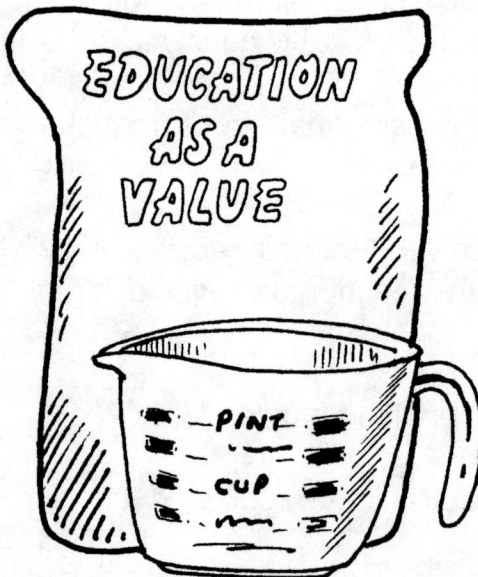

In order to achieve, you must **VALUE EDUCATION**. Your values are learned from others, such as your parents, friends, and teachers.

HOW TO GET GOOD GRADES

At Mel's party the other night Tim complained, "I don't know why you try to learn that there stuff. It never did me no good."

Mel agreed. "Listen, Tim. Education is worthless. Let's party!"

As the saying goes, "With friends like these, who needs enemies?" Perhaps you need friends like Lara and Alec:

"I'm studying extra hard in science," said Lara. "I think it's great we're learning about nature. It's opened up a whole new world for me."
Alec answered, "I really liked history today. We reviewed the Civil War and are planning to tour Gettysburg next month."

You get the idea?

If you want to improve your achievement in school, then pick friends who will support the value and worth of your learning experiences. You need positive reinforcement!

The first step in exploring a value is to become aware of it. Make a list of several of your close friends, your parents, teachers, and yourself. Beside each name, write a recent behavior that would indicate their belief in education. Remember, only our actions speak for our values.

HOW TO GET GOOD GRADES

Next, make a list of nine people – three professionals, such as nurses, judges, or engineers – three business people, perhaps a store manager, a salesperson, or the owner of a business – and three tradesmen, like a machinist, auto mechanic, or computer technician.

OPINIONS OF OTHERS HELP:

1. **APPRECIATE VALUES**
2. **INCREASE AWARENESS OF EDUCATION**
3. **PROVIDE REINFORCEMENT**
4. **SELF-MOTIVATION**

The opinions of others will help you to appreciate individual values as they relate to education. This will increase your awareness of education, and provide you with reinforcement and self-motivational material. Thus, the value of education could be to liberate your mind – to enable you to read, think, and act in a certain way.

Education is the road for social, economic, and mental improvement and satisfaction. Understanding its value will motivate you to achieve and improve your grades.

INGREDIENT #2

The second ingredient in our academic success mixture is **RELEVANCY**. Does this subject have meaning for you? Do you understand why it's important to learn this material? Does it meet your educational needs? Your school subjects have been designed to provide a general introduction or background of instruction which leads to more

8

specific learnings as you advance. Elementary, Middle, Junior High, High School and post-High School curriculum progress from broad to narrow – from general to specific. To learn, you must understand why the material is important, and what meaning it has for you. You must ask yourself, "Will I learn skills, facts, understandings, or appreciations studying this subject?"

Visit your career-resource room and school library to find career fields that require this subject.

When you understand how your courses relate to you and your future, you'll see a positive effect on your academic achievement and your grades.

Sometimes you might learn something for fun! When you feel positive about other subjects, you might relax and just enjoy learning.

INGREDIENT #3

If you **VALUE EDUCATION**, and see the **RELEVANCY** of your subjects, then you should learn the basic **SKILLS** of learning – so you can achieve! You wouldn't think of playing a game or weaving a basket without first learning the basic skills and rules and then practicing until you are successful. The skills that will help you are:

1. **TIME MANAGEMENT**
2. **HOW TO STUDY**
3. **HOW TO REMEMBER**
4. **HOW TO TAKE TESTS**

Let's take a brief look at each of them.

HOW TO GET GOOD GRADES

1. TIME MANAGEMENT

Parents often help children manage time. But time management becomes YOUR responsibility as you advance in school. With more freedom and so many new after-school activities, having a TIME BUDGET becomes very important.

HOURS NEEDED		
8 = sleep		
2 = meals		
2 = spent on bus	24	
_7_ = school	- 19	
19	5	

A simplified idea might be to add all the hours you know you'll need: Eight hours for sleep. Two more for meals. Two for transportation, and six to seven hours for school. The rest are available for homework and other events.

2. HOW TO STUDY

Knowing how to study is a broad topic. It requires you to improve your skills of listening, writing, and reading. You must learn how to take notes in class and from textbooks, and **LEARN THE ART OF REVIEWING**. Ask each subject teacher for tips on how to study for their course. Determine your learning style. Get together with a friend for review sessions.

3. HOW TO REMEMBER

Work on **IMPROVING YOUR MEMORY**. Read a paragraph or a page in a book, cover it up, and write down what you remembered. Read it out loud.

4. HOW TO TAKE TESTS

Learning is one side of the coin. Being able to demonstrate that learning is the other. Test-taking skills can be learned, and will increase your performance.

REDUCE TEST-TAKING ANXIETY by learning and practicing relaxing techniques such as self-sentences, deep breathing, tightening and relaxing your muscles. End with mental imagery; picture your favorite relaxing scene, such as being at the ocean and listening to the waves, or sitting in front of a blazing campfire.

By improving the skills associated with learning, you'll definitely increase your confidence and your self-esteem.

INGREDIENT #4

Learning and motivation are difficult to separate. Remember Mel telling Tim about Lara?

"We have a science test tomorrow, Tim. And you know Lara, if there's a test, she's got to study for it."

The questions we must answer are: What motivates us to study? And what motivates Tim's and Mel's behavior? Why are they content to party the night before a big science test?

| internal | external |

Motivation is a condition that activates our behavior and gives it direction. Motivation can be INTERNAL or EXTERNAL.

Lara's motivation was INTERNAL. She didn't go to the party, but stayed home and studied because she was INTERNALLY motivated. Psychologists refer to this as the locus of control. If our locus of control is INTERNAL, then we are in control of what happens to us. We motivate ourselves to act.

Remember Hal's words? "I failed. Why does everything happen to me?"

Hal has an EXTERNAL locus of control. He doesn't believe that he is in control of his motivations. He believes that they are controlled by fate, chance, or destiny. Hal can only be motivated to action by an EXTERNAL incentive, such as the fifty dollars that Tim's mother promised him if he got an A. Your locus of control is extremely difficult to change. So, we can become aware of how we are motivated and ride with the tide – or we can try to change it. Ideally, we want to become INTERNALLY motivated. The only real motivation is self-motivation. We are in charge of our actions and take full responsibility for them.

Lara has eliminated achievement anxiety, which has resulted in her positive-achievement motivation. She has the DESIRE to do well – to achieve!

Students are either motivated to achieve success, or to avoid failure. Some will work hard to get the A, while others will work to keep from getting the F.

And there's another factor that contributes to self-motivation.

"I'll probably get my usual D."

Tim's level of aspiration is low. He's not really motivated to study, learn, and achieve because, in the past, he hasn't been successful.

Success raises our future level of aspiration and failure lowers it. Persistent success or failure can raise or lower one's ambition, drive, or motivation.
Gaining, or regaining confidence once it's lost, is difficult. You need hard work and a few good grades on which to build. Remember, success breeds success.

So what's needed to achieve academic success? To acquire knowledge and to become educated must be something that you truly value. This educational value must be demonstrated by your actions. Education must be important to you. You must fully understand why it's important for you to study a particular subject. It must have meaning for you and be related to your future.

You must believe that you can achieve as well as, if not better than, others. However, you are not in competition with anyone except yourself. You must evaluate your progress against your own standards and not those of others. You are seeking self-improvement.

Sharpen your learning tools by improving your reading, note-taking, and listening skills. Practice time-management techniques and test-taking skills, and use study methods that fit your individual learning style.

You should establish learning goals and assume responsibility for reaching those goals.

What motivates you to action? And what techniques have you developed for self-motivation?

Set realistic levels of progress – high enough, but not too high. Try to improve your performance gradually. Don't reach or aspire too high at first.

HOW TO GET GOOD GRADES

Strive for consistency in achievement. Try and get into the A or B groove. Don't bounce from an A to an F. And don't slack off near the end of the term. The final grades mean as much as the earlier ones, but often require that "second wind."

Self-motivation is a must! If you shoot basketball, you say to yourself, *"I'm going to make that basket!"* That same kind of thinking is needed in school. Tell yourself, *"I'm going to work hard and get an A."* Positive thinking is a powerful tool, so use it to your advantage. However, you must follow this up with actions that will ensure success and above all, remember to use the 3-S solution to achievement: STUDY! STUDY! STUDY!

Then, when someone asks you what's needed to get good grades, you can say, "Good grades? It's as easy as baking a cake. All you need are the right ingredients."

Back in class, a message came over the loudspeaker: "Attention! Attention! The following students have made the honor roll this semester:

Hal Sachs
Tim Martin
Sue Briggs
Lara Smith..."

HOW TO GET GOOD GRADES

FILL IN THE BLANKS

Fill in the blank in each sentence with the correct word from the box below.

future	time
parents	general
value	reading
friends	relevancy

1. If you want to improve your achievement in school, pick

   _____ that support the value of learning

   and education.

2. In order to achieve in school, you must _____

   education.

3. Values are learned from teachers, friends, and

   _____.

4. For education to be important to you, it must have

   _____.

5. School and school subjects progress from

   _____ to specific.

6. Understanding how your courses relate to your

   _____ plans can improve your grades.

7. With so much freedom and so many activities, good grades

   are the result of proper_____ management.

8. The three skills needed for good grades are listening,

   writing, and _____.

Answers can be found on page 31.

15

HOW TO GET GOOD GRADES

DEFINE THE WORDS

Listed below are the four main ingredients needed for school achievement. Give a brief description of each.

1. EDUCATION AS A VALUE:_____

_____

_____

_____

2. RELEVANCY:_____

_____

_____

_____

3. LEARNING SKILLS:_____

_____

_____

_____

4. MOTIVATION: _____

_____

_____

_____

Suggested answers can be found on page 31.

MATCHING

Match Column A with Column B by writing the appropriate letter on the line.

COLUMN A	COLUMN B
_____ 1. internal motivation	A. not in control of actions
_____ 2. career field	B. raises level of aspirations
_____ 3. external motivation	C. liberates the mind
_____ 4. success	D. self-motivation
_____ 5. education	E. resource room / library

List three of your favorite school subjects.

1.

2.

3.

List three occupations you are considering.

OCCUPATION   NUMBER OF SCHOOL YEARS REQUIRED

1.

2.

3.

Answers can be found on page 31.

LEARNING
HOW TO STUDY

"Mr. Sanders, I just don't understand how I could have failed. I stayed up until 2:00 A.M. studying."

"Well, Mary," answered Mr. Sanders, "your test result doesn't seem to indicate that you studied very much."

"But I did, Mr. Sanders. I really did. I sure wish I knew what was wrong. Maybe it's my brain."

SOUND FAMILIAR?

Everything we do requires learning, whether it's basketball fundamentals, weaving on a loom, making something interesting, or fishing for the "big one."

LEARNING HOW TO STUDY

Studying seems to be the key to a great deal of learning. Let's review some of the basic rules for studying with Mr. Sanders.

"Today," begins Mr. Sanders, "I'd like to put our books aside. Mary has asked me to review some of the fundamentals for studying, and I think you all could benefit from them.
"There are five basic, but very closely related areas that each of you must be aware of, and master, if you're going to study effectively.

1. **Self-motivation**
2. **Time management**
3. **Self-knowledge**
4. **Improving the skills of**
   a. **listening**
   b. **note taking**
   c. **reading**
5. **Reviewing**

"Mr. Sanders, are they listed in their order of importance?" asked Dan.

"No, they aren't, but remember, I said that they are closely related.

"Studying is hard work. It requires a lot of determination and self-motivation on your part. You've got to be motivated to *want* to study. This motivation can only be achieved by YOU. To learn to advance – to achieve – you must study!"

"But, Mr. Sanders, I stayed up until 2:00 A.M. the night before the test and I still failed!" said Mary.

"Staying up late and studying are two different things, Mary. None of the material on this last test was that hard. I believe you need some help with managing your time.

"Each of you must plan your study time. YOU know when the tests are going to be given, so plan to study a few hours each day.

"Then the night before the test, you can go to bed at ten o'clock."

JULY						
MONDAY	TUESDAY	WED.	THURSDAY	FRIDAY	SATURDAY	SUNDAY
1	2	3	4	5	6	7
8	9	10	11	12	13	14
15	16	17	18	19	20	21
22	23	24	25	26	27	28
29	30	31				

"My mom says she used to get up at five o'clock on the morning of her big test to study. She said it was quiet, and she was mentally alert," said Mark.

LEARNING HOW TO STUDY

Mr. Sanders smiled. "Yes, that's a good idea. Many of our early scholars did this. However, it might not be for everybody. That's why it's important for you to KNOW SOMETHING ABOUT YOURSELF. Think about your likes and dislikes. Do you like to study alone, or with a friend? In a quiet, isolated area? Or in an open, well-lighted area?

"You must decide how you like to study and then plan to study on a regular schedule. And don't fool yourself — make wise use of your study time. Some of you might study better in small groups. This is often a great way to review for a test.

"Some of you can study *anywhere*, and seem to enjoy it. However, most of us need well-lighted rooms and straight chairs to prevent fatigue — and to be where help for difficult problems can easily be obtained.

"The next item I'd like to discuss is LISTENING.

"I refer to this as a skill because, with practice, it can be improved. Some say that through our ears we learn as much as 85% of what we know. But our minds can function much faster than we can talk, so it's important to concentrate on what's being said. If you don't...

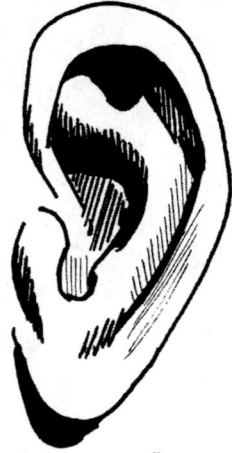

you'll drift away.

"This leads us into the skill of NOTETAKING. Taking notes not only will help you when it's time to review, but it will also keep your mind tuned to the class. When the teacher writes something down on the board,

you should write it down in your notes. When the teacher stresses a point, you should write it down. This way, you'll be able to review it before a test – and you won't forget it.

$$\begin{array}{r} 9 \\ \times\,5 \\ \hline 95 \end{array}$$

"When you take notes, make sure they are clear and readable. Don't try to get everything word for word. Be brief. If you are taking notes from the board and you don't understand something, that's the time to ask your teacher. If you don't understand, or your notes are wrong, you'll probably get it wrong on the test.

"Now, the final skill I want to discuss with you is READING.

"Most of our formal or school learning is based on reading. Now, as both you and I know, some of us are fast readers and some of us are slow readers. Some remember everything they read the first time they read it – and others have to re-read material several times before they remember. Don't worry about this, but you must know your reading style and you must identify it.

"When you are finished reading a page, cover the page, and try to write down several facts . This will help you remember what you've read. And remember, when you are reading,

you can't be listening to music,

or become too comfortable. Because soon, your eyes will close and you'll be in Dreamville.

"A good way to improve your reading skills is to go to the library and find a good book. Make certain it's something you're interested in, and it's not too hard for you to read.

"Reading, like all skills, can be improved by practice.

"Now, the last area I want to cover for you today is REVIEWING.

"Some teachers say that all studying is really reviewing. By now, each of you have motivated yourselves to study, carefully planned your study time, and are working on your study and learning skills. It doesn't matter if the teacher gave you an assignment or not, you must plan to study each day. Get into the study habit. Use that time to re-read important chapters or take notes from the textbook. You know, some students will outline every chapter, so when it's time to review, they're ready.

"For the last five minutes of your review period, read your notes, cover them with your hand, and see how much you can remember. After several days of doing this, you'll be the brightest student in the room!"

Being smart is knowing the rules for studying – and following them! When time runs out,

you'll be the winner! In more ways than one.

LEARNING HOW TO STUDY

TRUE (T) or FALSE (F)

_____1. All students learn at the same time.

_____2. Eating habits do not affect learning.

_____3. Reviewing is one of the most important aspects of learning.

_____4. Some students learn more quickly by listening than by reading.

_____5. Taking class notes is an art that must be mastered for effective learning.

TIME MAP

Knowing how much time we have to set aside for learning is important. There is a need to see how we spend our time and look for better ways to manage it. A time map of four to five days will help us. Make several lists. Include **MUST-DO** items such as household chores, work, school, study, and **MAY-DO** items such as television, phone time, and activities. Then look for **WASTE-TIME** items.

TIME MAP

	Day 1	Day 2	Sat.	Sun.
6:00 A.M.	get up & look for clothes		sleeping	sleeping
7:00 A.M.	eat breakfast		↓	↓
8:00 A.M.	school-first class		soccer practice	shower/dress
9:00 A.M.	↓		↓	church
10:00 A.M.				
11:00 A.M.	↓		↓	brunch
12:00 P.M.	lunch		home/lunch	
1:00 P.M.	classes			relax/read
2:00 P.M.				newspaper/
3:00 P.M.	↓			watch sports
4:00 P.M.	home-list chores			on television
5:00 P.M.				
6:00 P.M.	dinner			dinner
7:00 P.M.	study			study for test
8:00 P.M.	↓			in history
9:00 P.M.				
10:00 P.M.	bedtime			

Answers can be found on page 32.

FOOD MAP

Food affects our body chemistry and, as a result, our learning. Make a list of all the food and drink you consume for three days. Be sure to include snacks and the type of liquid: water, milk, juice, or soda.

FILL IN THE BLANKS WITH THESE WORDS:

time	Reviewing
Notes	listening
themselves	motivation
practice	groups

1. Studying requires a lot of self-_____.

2. _____ must be clear and readable.

3. Reading can be improved with _____.

4. Some say that by _____, we learn as much as 85% of what we know.

5. Managing _____ is necessary for learning.

6. _____all notes before a test will result in a higher grade.

7. Some students can learn more quickly when studying by _____, while others like _____.

Answers can be found on page 32.

CROSSWORD PUZZLE

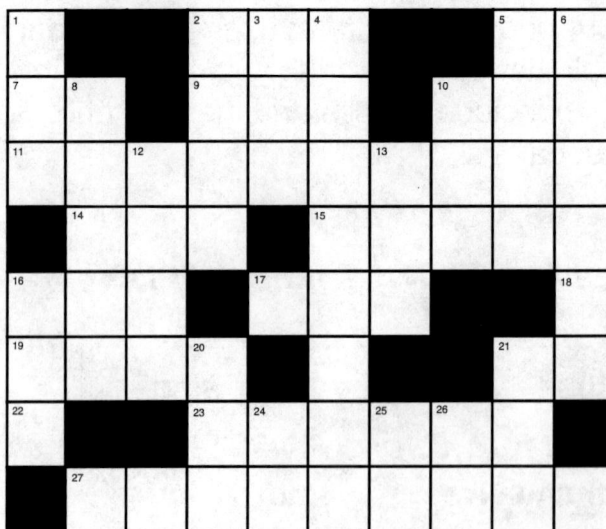

ACROSS

1. 13th letter
2. Road _____
   (shows you where you are)
5. 4th note of musical scale
7. Not off
9. Reconstruct music, abbr.
10. Not against
11. A feeling that makes one
    take action
14. Metal used for cans
15. _____van, a fine leather
16. Precious stone
17. Consumed
18. 12ᵗʰ letter
19. Secondhand; old
21. Mr. _____, T.V. horse
22. Same as 1 across
23. Quiet place to study
27. Looking over again

DOWN

1. Famous maker of apple pie
2. Most important idea
3. American revised version, abbr.
4. _____ makes perfect
5. Affects our body chemistry and
   our learning
6. Mr. Schwarzenegger
8. Make these clear and readable
10. Kind of evergreen tree
12. A clock tells you this
13. Division of the foot
16. Chewing _____
20. Disabled Amer. Veteran, abbr.
21. Even, in poetry
24. 51 in Roman numerals
25. Cry of pain
26. Virgin Islands, abbr.

Answers can be found on page 32.

ANSWER KEY

HOW TO GET GOOD GRADES

FILL IN THE BLANKS

1. friends
2. value
3. parents
4. relevancy

5. general
6. future
7. time
8. reading

DEFINE THE WORDS (Suggested Answers)

1. To be aware of the value of an education. Associate with friends who value an education and who will support your efforts.

2. Does a particular subject have meaning for you? Understanding the importance of learning a particular subject. Does it meet your educational needs? Understanding how certain subjects relate to you and your future.

3. Time management; How to study; How to remember; How to take tests

4. Motivation is the internal will to succeed – the desire to do well. Self-motivation puts you in control of your future.

MATCHING

1. D
2. E
3. A
4. B
5. C

ANSWER KEY

LEARNING HOW TO STUDY

TRUE OR FALSE

1. F
2. F
3. T
4. T
5. T

FILL IN THE BLANKS

1. motivation
2. Notes
3. practice
4. listening
5. time
6. Reviewing
7. themselves, groups

CROSSWORD PUZZLE

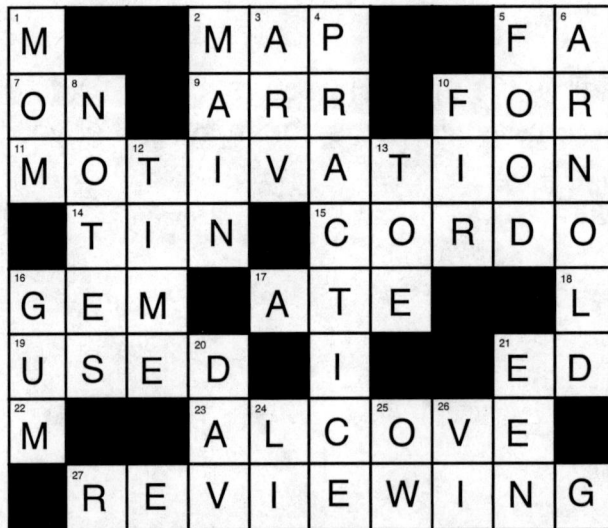

¹M	■	²M	³A	⁴P	■	⁵F	⁶A
⁷O	⁸N	■	⁹A	R	R	■	¹⁰F	O	R
¹¹M	O	¹²T	I	V	A	¹³T	I	O	N
■	¹⁴T	I	N	■	¹⁵C	O	R	D	O
¹⁶G	E	M	■	¹⁷A	T	E	■	¹⁸L
¹⁹U	S	E	²⁰D	■	I	■	²¹E	D
²²M	■	■	²³A	²⁴L	C	²⁵O	²⁶V	E	■
■	²⁷R	E	V	I	E	W	I	N	G

32